Warm in Winter Cool in Summer

Our house

This is our house.

Winter

When it is cold outside,
we can keep
our house warm inside.

5

Pink batts

Look at these.

They will help to keep our house warm inside.

Sausage dog

Look at this.
This goes at the door.
It will help to keep
our house warm inside.

Summer

When it is hot outside,
we can keep
our house cool inside.

Curtains

Look at the **curtains.**

We will close the curtains

on a hot day.

Closing the curtains will

help to keep

our house cool inside.

Verandah

Look at the **verandah.**

It will help to keep

our house cool inside.

Glossary

curtains

verandah